My Smart Infant

SMARTGUIDE
NEWBORN TO 6 MONTHS

The Inside Scoop on What It Takes to Enhance Your Baby's Learning Capacity

BONNIE ROSENSTEIN, M.A. Ed.

mySmartChild Series: age-related SmartGuides for parents to enhance their child's learning development ranging from infant through the elementary school years and beyond.

Although every precaution has been taken to verify the accuracy of the information contained herein, the author and publisher assume no responsibility for any errors or omissions. No liability is assumed for damages that may result from the use of information contained within. If you have any questions regarding the appropriateness of any of the information in this book, please consult with your child's pediatrician.

Note: This book utilizes third-person plural pronouns in the gender-neutral, singular sense.

Published by:
Mom's Campus Inc.
BOCA RATON, FL 33433

Copyright © 2018, 2023 by Bonnie Rosenstein. All rights reserved.

ISBN: 978-0-69214-509-8

No part of this book may be reproduced in any written, electronic, recording, or photocopying without written permission of the publisher or author. The exception would be in the case of brief quotations embodied in the critical articles or reviews and pages where permission is specifically granted by the publisher or author.

Production by The Book Couple • www.thebookcouple.com

*To Rich . . . my husband, for his love, support,
ideas, and encouraging me to write this book*

*To Jett and Britt . . . my amazing and talented
kids, my model students, and my inspiration*

*To Mom and Dad . . . for suggesting that I become
a teacher and for always being there for me*

Contents

Foreword................................1

About mySmartChild Book Series................3

Overview of My Smart Infant................5

Welcome to mySmartChild................7

You and Your New Baby................9

Infant Development Checklist (3 to 6 months)........10

Essential Tips & Information for a Well-Rounded Baby..14

Suggested Toys and Items for the Home............20

Establishing Baby-Safe Enrichment Areas
in the Home................28

Learning Activities (Newborn to 6 Months)..........30

    Bubbles, Bubbles Everywhere................31

    Can You Find It?................32

    Tummy Time!................33

    Mirror, Mirror. 34

    Touch and Feel. 35

    Buzzing World of Words. 36

    Dancing to the Music 37

    Pop! Goes the Weasel 38

    Look Who's Here! 39

    Kicking Back 40

Fostering Positive Qualities. 41

Age-Appropriate Storybooks (Newborn to
6 Months & Older) 44

To Sum It All Up 46

Testimonials 47

About Bonnie Rosenstein, M.A. Ed. 48

Foreword

Parenting an infant is one part joy, one part terror, and a whole lot of mystery. There's so much to "know" . . . and then there are so many things that you don't know. Once past the drying of the nursery paint, the gestation period, and the excitement of our children's birth, it becomes apparent to each of us that, in many respects, we're lovingly in over our heads. We soon discover just how little time we have to resolve questions about the emotional and intellectual development of our children while in the day-to-day feeding and diaper-changing trenches of new parenthood.

Even when cognizant of a general sense of missing something, we continue to triage food, clothing, and shelter, sleepily hoping that we are inadvertently meeting our child's "other" needs. It is the sweet exhaustion attendant to the routinization of parenting that masks the underlying fear that there are those "things" we aren't attending to . . . or that we haven't, can't, or don't resolve . . . because we're simply too sleep deprived to manage it. Admittedly, when the effect on our children isn't immediately clear, it is, sometimes, difficult to care.

That's where Bonnie, our new best friend, comes in. She's been there and done that and done it well. I have long admired her (and husband, Rich's) work. I know her smart, talented, and accomplished children. With this book, Bonnie has produced an invaluable resource for new parents that take the guesswork and anxiety out of developmental stewardship. The book is an accessibly concise treasure trove of information that educates and assists the new parent, as well as the most seasoned "veteran," with a better understanding of how we can foster the emotional and intellectual development of our children without the exorbitant graduate school tuition and caffeine-fueled all-nighters.

We're in good hands here. This has been Bonnie's life's work and a labor of love for her. Let the adventure begin.

Frank J. Mulhall, Esq.
Attorney and Social Commentator

About mySmartChild Book Series

The mySmartChild book series is a much-needed, high-quality resource for parents of young children who want to learn more effective ways to teach their children the basic skills needed for their age group and how to strengthen their child's current skills for higher learning.

The home is an important learning environment. A strong foundation at home is imperative academically, socially, and emotionally for every child. The main focus of mySmartChild is to provide educational strategies to help parents of children ranging in age from newborn to elementary age to enrich and foster a strong foundation of skills. To help children succeed in life, parents need to provide a loving, warm, and secure environment in the home, as well as an educational and enriching atmosphere. From the moment a baby is born, the mySmartChild resources are available to help parents prepare their children for school and successful academic achievement.

Some parents don't know what their child should be achieving at their current age level, where to access educational materials, or how to utilize the materials they do have. Moreover, many parents may not have the time to work with their child and simply need to figure out how to incorporate the teaching opportunities into their daily routines. This is where the mySmartChild guides can make an important difference.

My Smart Infant, the first book in the series, coaches parents specifically on how to set up and design an enriching learning environment in the home and how to utilize educational products to teach their children. The SmartGuide books are designed for children on all learning levels and ages. SmartGuides are useful for the new baby who is just beginning to learn and discover the world, the baby who needs developmental activities to grow and learn, the child who is developing at a standard rate, the child who needs extra help, and for the above-average child who needs more enrichment and advancement.

The SmartGuides coach and train parents so they will have the know-how to teach their children and enhance their education. When you start using mySmartChild resources early on with your baby, you will be amazed by how confident and successful your child becomes.

If you think your child may be headed in the direction of a gifted and talented student and your goal is to help them get into a gifted school program in elementary or middle school, we can help you. Be on the lookout for other educational materials for the "gifted child."

Look for other age-related SmartGuides, educational products, and ideas here:

 facebook.com/mySmartChild (and Facebook group)

 Instagram@mySmartChild

We offer VIRTUAL one-on-one and group parent sessions. Reach out on social media for a *FREE* consultation.

Overview of My Smart Infant

DESIGNED FOR: Babies from newborn to 6 months

FOR USE BY: Parents looking to provide a stimulating and safe environment where their baby can begin to explore and learn.

WHAT'S COVERED?

Developmental Age-related Checklist

This is a checklist of milestones that can be used as a guide for growth and development of your baby.

Essential Tips & Information

Raising children is not an easy task. In today's world, it is a great challenge to raise children. This SmartGuide for infants will help make this task a little easier. Having a baby is one part, but taking care of and educating that baby is a great challenge. This SmartGuide focuses on the positive side of raising children. Find out how to play with your baby, when to read to them, what to say to them, and so on.

Toys & Items for the Home

With the right resources, gathering the suggested toys and items can be done inexpensively. Knowing what to stock in your home to help your baby learn and to love learning is crucial. Some of the most important supplies are items most people already keep around the house.

How to Create and Set Up an Enriching Learning Environment

Examples include colors, shapes, and patterns and what you should have around your child's room and what you can do to stimulate their mind.

Learning Activities

These are age-appropriate activities for you to engage in with your baby.

Ways to Develop Self-esteem and Various Positive Qualities

Self-esteem is your child's passport to a lifetime of mental health and social happiness. It is the foundation of a child's well-being and the key to success as an adult. At all ages, how we feel about ourselves affects how we act. Think about a time when you were feeling good about yourself. You probably found it much easier to get along with others and feel good about your interactions. Of course, you want to foster this in your child from the beginning.

Resources

Suggested list of age-appropriate storybooks.

Welcome to mySmartChild

A parent is a child's first and most important teacher.

The most important years in a child's life are the first three years. The brain never grows more rapidly and dramatically than it does during those years. A child's most important learning experience will not come from video games, movies, or apps on a smartphone or iPad, but from interactions with those who care about them most—parents and/or guardians.

A parent is a child's first and most important teacher, not because they teach the alphabet, shapes, and colors, but because they encourage and motivate the child's curiosity and enthusiasm to learn. A parent helps a child to take in as much as they can learn from their environment by gently buffering them from sometimes more than they can handle. On the other hand, a child can teach their parents how to read their cues so that together they can work toward a great balance between learning and fun.

We are living in a world of growing technology, but I truly believe that we all need to go back to basics with our children sometimes. Children still need the hands-on approach to learning. You can still use smartphones, computers, tablets like iPads, videos, and apps, but only use them as a supplement. Even though our children today are living in the age of fast-moving technological advances, I really hope they learn to take the time to appreciate the simpler, but more profound, things in life.

As parents, we initially want to prepare our home to be safe and nurturing. With those essential elements in place, we can also create a stimulating learning environment in the home. This SmartGuide will educate you on the appropriate materials and activities to help you prepare your child for school and for life. It's never too early to get on the road to great academic success!

A strong educational foundation in the home starts a child off in the right direction and leads them through years of successful schooling. You hold the future of this person entirely in your hands. What your child becomes depends largely on you! They are born a "blank slate" so it's up to you to guide them at the beginning as soon as they are born. Raise your child with love and understanding. Stimulate their brain at every opportunity, and they will find learning easy and fun throughout their lives.

I know you are busy or may work long hours, but when you have some special quality time with your child, do the activities suggested. You can also have a grandparent, babysitter/nanny, friend, or anyone who watches your baby use this SmartGuide. If you can use this SmartGuide from day one and get into the habit and routine of doing even one suggested activity daily, your baby will benefit. Once you get into a routine with this SmartGuide, you will see that your child will be "one step ahead" in their overall growth.

A smart learning path begins at home.

Bonnie Rosenstein, M.A. Ed.
Founder and Chief Education Officer of mySmartChild
President of Mom's Campus Inc.

You and Your New Baby

Congratulations on bringing your newborn home! This is an exciting time for you and your family. For the first three months (**from newborn to 3 months**), you and your baby will develop a deep bond fostered by unconditional love. Mostly, during this time, your baby will be eating/drinking, crying, excreting, and sleeping. However, your baby will experience some moments of alertness.

A baby's brain is ready to take in everything, which makes every experience your baby has important. Go ahead and talk to your baby, hold them close, and rock them to sleep. You can even begin to read aloud to them. They grow up fast, and before you know it, you'll be ready to begin implementing more of the suggestions in this book . . . and beyond. But, most of all, enjoy your time with your newborn!

Infant Development Checklist (3 to 6 months)

Every baby develops at their own pace, so it is impossible to tell exactly when your child will learn a given skill. The developmental steps listed below provide a *general* idea of the changes you can expect, but don't be alarmed if your baby's development is not exactly as listed. This checklist is not set in stone; it is just a guide. The skills may vary for each baby by a few months.

If you notice anything unusual with your baby's development, please speak with your child's doctor. Nevertheless, if you understand which skills and abilities a baby normally develops by a specific age, you will be equipped to educate your baby by stimulating them with the right toys and materials for that level.

The Third Month

- **Holding head steady.** During this month, your baby may be able to lift their head while on their back and hold it for several minutes. If sitting with support, they may be able to hold their head steady and erect. When they are on their stomach, you might see them lifting their head and chest as if they are doing mini-pushups. You can offer encouragement by sitting in front of the baby and dangling a toy.

❏ **Better arm, leg, and hand coordination.** Your baby may now wave their arms and kick their legs. As their hip and knee joints become more flexible, their kicks are getting stronger. And if you hold them up with their feet on the floor, they should push down on their legs now. They can bring both hands together and open their fingers, though they'll probably use a closed fist to bat at dangling objects. (Of course, swatting at a toy or other object is developmental progress in itself!) Encourage their hand development by holding out a toy to see if they'll grasp it.

❏ **Sleeping patterns getting more manageable.** Starting about now, sleep-deprived parents may get some relief. By 3 to 4 months, your child's sleep patterns may start to settle down. Many babies this age can even sleep through the night, though they may still wake up for the occasional feeds. But some children may not sleep through the night (which, for the first year, usually means just six hours at a time), for a good three to six months, so don't worry if your baby still keeps you up at night.

❏ **Clear recognition of Mom and Dad.** By three months, and probably earlier, your baby will have formed an attachment to you and be familiar with your face. Most likely they will still smile at strangers, especially when the strangers look straight in the baby's eye and coo or talk to them. But they are beginning to sort out who's who in their life and prefer some people to others. The parietal lobe, the part of the brain that governs hand-eye coordination and allows a person to recognize objects, is developing rapidly now. And the temporal lobe, which assists with hearing, language, and smell, has also become more receptive and active. So, when your baby hears your voice now, they may look directly at you and start gurgling or trying to talk back.

The Fourth Month

- ❏ Drooling begins
- ❏ Good head control
- ❏ May sit with support
- ❏ Bears some weight on legs when held upright
- ❏ Raises head and chest off surface to a 90-degree angle
- ❏ Rolls from back to side
- ❏ Explores and plays with hands
- ❏ Tries to reach for objects but overshoots
- ❏ Grasps objects with both hands
- ❏ Eye-hand coordination begins
- ❏ Makes consonant sounds
- ❏ Laughs
- ❏ Enjoys being rocked, bounced, or swung

The Fifth Month

- ❏ Signs of teething begin
- ❏ Holds head up when sitting
- ❏ Rolls from stomach to back
- ❏ When lying on back, puts feet to mouth
- ❏ Voluntarily grasps and holds objects
- ❏ Plays with toes
- ❏ Takes objects directly to mouth

- ❏ Watches objects that are dropped
- ❏ Says "ah-goo" or similar vowel-consonant combinations
- ❏ Smiles at mirror image
- ❏ Gets upset if you take away a toy
- ❏ Can tell family and strangers apart
- ❏ Begins to discover parts of their body

The Sixth Month

- ❏ Chewing and biting occur
- ❏ When on stomach can lift chest and part of stomach off the surface, bearing weight on hands
- ❏ Lifts head when pulled to a sitting position
- ❏ Rolls from back to stomach
- ❏ Bears majority of weight when being held in a standing position
- ❏ Grasps and controls small objects
- ❏ Holds bottle
- ❏ Grabs feet and pulls to mouth
- ❏ Adjusts body to see an object
- ❏ Turns head from side to side and then looks up or down
- ❏ May be able to sit without support
- ❏ Prefers more complex visual stimuli
- ❏ Says one syllable sounds like "ma," "mu," "da," and "di"
- ❏ Recognizes parents

Essential Tips & Information for a Well-Rounded Baby

Before your baby reaches 3 months of age, the most important thing you can do is simply to love your child unconditionally. Cuddle, coo, smile, and talk to your baby as often as possible. The more often you do these things, the more wonderful the first three months will be! The following are some important tips and information you will want to keep in mind and incorporate as soon as your baby enters your home; other ideas here pertain to older infants (and sometimes toddlers). Above all, enjoy the time you have with your child as you foster growth and learning.

Decorate the room with your baby in mind.

Keep pastel colors to a minimum in your baby's room in the beginning. Newborn babies need bright, bold contrasting colors to attract their attention and to stimulate their growing brains, so design a colorful room with big bold, eye-catching shapes and patterns. Young babies enjoy looking at shapes and patterns and will learn from them. Babies like to gaze at black, white, and some red patterns.

Spend time gazing at your child.

Studies on babies show that they like looking at the human face and their mom's face. They respond to human faces by staring at them. They prefer faces to anything else. Engage in many one-to-one, face-to-face interactions with your baby. While doing so, use simple language and frequent eye contact.

Start reading to your newborn baby right away and read aloud to your baby every day.

Reading to a child, no matter how young, will pay off. It helps your baby develop an ear for the cadence of language—in fact, varying the pitch of your voice, using accents, singing, and vocalizing make the aural connection between you and your baby much more stimulating. But don't worry if your baby looks the other way or loses concentration—adjust their stimulation by trying something else, or give them time to rest. Try to coordinate your interactions with their responses and interest.

There are plenty of good books to read to your baby. Choose board books with large, bright pictures and simple text—or even wordless books with pictures for you to narrate. You can check out a few books from your local library, purchase them from bookstores or websites, or borrow books from a neighbor or friend. (For some recommended storybooks, see page 44.)

At this point, you shouldn't be so strict with the age guidelines. Books designed for older children with clear, crisp images and bright colors can captivate your baby. Or you can read poetry originally written for adult ears. What they don't understand will nonetheless delight your baby because of its musicality.

Please, no baby talk (early language development).

This is a sensitive time when verbal stimulation is particularly important for your baby. Seize the moment and engage your baby with a variety of words and sounds. Recent research links higher intelligence levels to how many words a child hears in the first year of life. This is the time to set a sound foundation. Speak in full sentences, naming everything around you. Even a trip to the store can be a chance to stimulate your baby: as you roam the aisles, point to objects and identify them by name and color. Even though your baby can't yet repeat these words, they are storing all the information in their rapidly developing memory.

Embrace your bilingual home.

A baby in a bilingual home will get double the language training if they regularly hear both languages spoken. If you'd like your child to learn more than one language, have each parent speak to the baby in a different language. Please note this will be a very positive experience for them to know multiple languages.

Stimulate your baby's sense of touch, which is becoming more sensitive.

Look for materials such as fur, tissue, felt, and terry cloth or for books that make touching part of the reading experience. Touching, carrying, and massaging your baby, along with moving them through the air when you lift them, are powerful ways to relax your baby and may even increase their alertness and attention span.

Foster interaction with others.

Your child is set to "receive" and draws conclusions about the world around them. By now, they may respond to their face in the mirror by smiling (babies love looking at themselves), and they may stop sucking their thumb or bottle to listen to your voice. By cooing or making noises at them and by describing even the most mundane household chore, you're not only connecting with your baby but also encouraging them to express themselves. Even with others, your baby is becoming more animated and engaging—flashing smiles, oohing, and cooing. The fun has really begun. When you're with friends, keep the baby nearby so they can hear the richness of human interaction.

Play music often.

Spending time with your baby while music is playing is a wonderful opportunity to enhance your parent-child bond. Music can be relaxing for your baby. It also stimulates your baby's mind and physical development. Classical music, such as symphonies by Mozart and Beethoven, are very stimulating for babies' brains. Your baby may also enjoy some current songs and even your old favorites, if the music and lyrics are not too loud or distracting. Musical resources are abundant on the Internet (such as YouTube) or from music apps on your smartphone or use a Bluetooth speaker for your music from your phone or tablet; you can even use music channels on your TV.

Sing to your baby.

Singing to your baby shows them that you are interested in them. Some great song choices to sing to your baby include classic lullabies. The reason is that this music is often simple and repetitive, making it helpful for the development of communication skills. Some examples are "Baa, Baa, Black Sheep" (an English nursery rhyme), "Swing Low, Sweet Chariot" (an African-American spiritual song), "Twinkle, Twinkle, Little Star" and "Hush, Little Baby" (both popular English lullabies). Also, your baby will enjoy nursery rhymes such as "Jack and Jill," "Humpty Dumpty," and "Little Bo Peep." You can find these songs and nursery rhymes with words in books from a bookstore or local library or you can do a Google search for websites that include them. Also, YouTube has great videos and music that sing to you or you can sing along. Additionally, there are free apps you can download on your smartphone or tablet.

If you feel like the above lullabies and rhymes are too old fashioned (no worries; they are even outdated for me), just sing any of your favorite songs from your own playlist. Anything you choose to sing will be appreciated by your baby. Just hearing your voice is enough, and it doesn't even have to be good. I can't sing in tune . . . so it is all good.

Pack a board book.

Whenever you leave the house, always bring along a board book—that is, a book printed on thick paperboard used for both the cover and interior so that the pages will not tear. Board books usually have pictures or photos along with descriptive words for each image. If you have a few minutes of downtime while running errands and/or between appointments, go through the pages of the book with your baby or allow your baby to hold the book. Please do not resort to the habit of handing your baby your smartphone for stimulation. A good book is still the better choice.

Talk to your baby often, ask questions, and listen and respond to the sounds they make.

Children can develop language skills only if they have many opportunities to talk, listen, and use language to solve problems and learn about the world. Begin listening to your child's verbalizations right away and respond to their verbalizations to help foster two-way communication. Directly involve your baby in what's going on by talking to them before, during, and after moving them from place to place. Be especially attentive to infants during routines such as diaper changing, feeding, and changing clothes. Explain to your baby what will happen, what is happening, and what will happen next.

Additionally, asking your baby questions is a good way for your child to learn to compare and to classify things. (Although this does not pertain to ages 3 to 6 months, encourage older children to try to find the answer to their own questions. If you and your child don't know the answer—say so, and together, try to find the answer. If you do know the answer, however, it is very important for you, as a parent, to share it with your child.) All interactions should be characterized by gentle, supportive responses. Above all, listen and respond to sounds that your baby makes, imitate these sounds, and respect these sounds as the beginning of communication.

Be realistic about your baby's abilities and interests.

Set high standards and encourage your child as they get older to try new things. Children who aren't challenged become bored. But children who are pushed too quickly or who are asked to do things that don't interest them can become frustrated and unhappy.

Provide opportunities for your baby to do new things and experience a variety of places.

The more varied the experience your baby has, the more they will learn about the world. No matter where you live, your community can provide stimulating experiences. For example, go for frequent walks in your neighborhood and visit museums, libraries, zoos, and other places of interest. If you live in the city, spend a day in the suburbs. If you live in the suburbs, spend a day in the city.

Encourage your baby to be expressive.

In the early months, this will be in the form of vocalizations and body movements, but as your child gets older, provide the tools to allow your baby to make music, dance to music, paint, and so on. Let your child participate in many activities that help to develop their imagination and let them express their ideas and feelings as they develop through the years.

Suggested Toys and Items for the Home

There are many varieties of the toys suggested in the chart beginning on page 22. These are simply ideas to use as a starting point. Keep in mind, there are many other types of toys out there. In general, toys that are provided for three months and up should be responsive to the child's actions, such as musical toys, Jack in the Box, vinyl-covered soft pillows, large beads that snap together, small blocks, music boxes, and squeeze toys that squeak. They should also be scaled to a size that enables infants to grasp, chew, and manipulate such as sensory balls, rattles, teethers, and rubber bath toys.

When your baby begins to crawl and eventually toddlers who are walking, make their toys available on low, open shelves so they can make their own selections easily and independently. Please always watch your baby and small children carefully for safety reasons during playtime. Please note that the age ranges in the chart are guides; your baby may or may not be able to perform the skills stated at that time and that is okay. Each baby develops at their own pace.

A NOTE ABOUT TOYS AND OTHER ITEMS

Babies learn by playing. The items shown on the following pages are for **newborns, infants,** and **beyond.** These toys and items stimulate and encourage the development of specific skills at different months. In reviewing the list, you might be concerned that acquiring all of these items will be expensive. Be assured that these are suggestions for you to choose from. You don't need all of them; there are always options.

You may already have some of these items in your home, friends or family members whose children have outgrown their toys may give you theirs, and you can make them yourself or get them at low costs from a discount store or online. Make sure that whatever you get, make, or purchase is safe to use with infants before offering it. If you are purchasing a used item online, ask lots of questions about the condition of the item before you make the purchase.

You can simply do the best you can with the items you already have. For example, wooden spoons or even empty plastic containers make great "play" items. Your baby will still be very prepared and "one step ahead" in their overall growth development. You not only care and love your baby, but you are also educating them.

	NEWBORN & UP	
Black-and-white or brightly colored contrasting objects or toys with geometrical patterns. 	These items present the highest possible contrast to the eye and thus are the most visible and attractive to babies, especially up to 3 months. As they grow, they will enjoy more primary colors. Then a blend of contrasting colors and bright primary colors will provide further stimulation to your baby's environment.	
Black-and-White Picture Cards    	Black-and-white images stimulate babies' vision. According to Dr. Bill Sears, "A newborn retina can only detect large contrasts between light and dark, or black and white. So, while an adult can appreciate various shades of pastel colors on the walls of baby's room, a newborn may only see them as one shade all blurred together."* Pictures can be store-bought picture cards, or you can print baby-friendly black-and-white pictures such as symbols and animals from your computer. *https://www.askdrsears.com/topics/parenting/child-rearing-and-development/bright-starts-babys-development-through-interactive-play/playtime-articles/visual-stimulation-newborns	
Music 	For listening, brain development, and enjoyment. Music can soothe, especially lullabies and classical music. However, almost all music has great benefits. For instance, music makes babies feel good and helps build a bond between you and your baby. If you play music that you enjoy, you'll have more fun listening and singing along with your baby. That can also help with child development and preparation for school.	

3 MONTHS AND UP

Activity Mats 	Helps develop sensory skills and cause and effect (an action and its outcome). In the photo, the baby is grasping the hanging toy and sees it move. Lying on their back will help your baby's leg and arm muscles move the dangling toys. When they can roll over, tummy time is great for strengthening neck and shoulder muscles. Activity mats are great mostly between ages 3 and 6 months.
Famous "Boppy" Nursing Pillow/"U-shaped" soft pillow 	Great for tummy time and helps your baby with learning to sit. You can find this item at Amazon.com under "Nursing Boppy Pillow," other online retailers, or at local baby stores. This is great mostly between ages 3 and 6 months.
Mirror 	Helps your baby learn how to focus, track images, and explore the wonderful things a face can do. It also promotes social and emotional development. It's good for tummy time too! Make sure that any mirror you place in your baby's play area or crib is made from **plastic** and has a soft backing.
Ring Rattles 	Easy-to-grasp handle encourages your baby to bring their hands together, which is an important developmental milestone. This is great mostly between ages 3 and 6 months.

Bouncer Seat 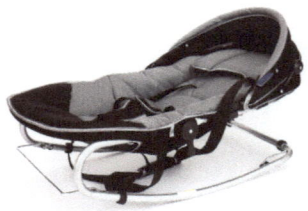	Seat gently bounces in response to your baby's natural motions. Some have buttons to turn on calming vibrations, too. When it's time to play, some seats encourage your baby to reach and grasp dangling toys (exercising and developing motor skills). May be used for "Bubbles" activity (see page 31).
Textured Water-Filled Teethers 	Multiple textures inside and outside to stimulate gums. (Chill water teether in refrigerator for cooling effect.) Make sure the teether is BPA-free, contains no phthalates, and is filled with non-toxic liquid. Always wash in hot, soapy water and rinse well after each use.

4 MONTHS AND UP

Bubbles 	Bubbles have many benefits, such as development of gross motor skills and eye/hand coordination. Your baby may look and follow the bubbles around, which is great for tracking. Older infants may try to reach for and pop the bubbles, and toddlers may reach way up high, stand on their tippy toes, squat, jump, run, stomp, and kick. The toddler years are when they may begin to blow their own.
Jack in the Box 	This toy will bring a smile to your baby's face. Until your baby gets older, you turn the handle to hear the fun song and *POP!*—an adorable plush figure pops out! Push the toy back in, close the lid, and start the fun. This toy is an example of cause and effect: an action or event that will produce a certain response to the action (cranking the handle to see the toy pop up). When your baby gets older (approximately within their first year), they will love to crank the handle themselves.

Open/Shut Toys 	For hands, fingers, and for exploring. You may use any safe box with a lid, containers, hard sunglass cases, jewelry boxes, or music boxes. You may want to model this activity for your baby to show them how to open and close a lid. By observing you often, your baby will eventually be able to perform the skill themselves.
Puppets 	When the puppet is animated by you, you can engage your baby in language development and communication. Brightly colored puppets with engaging eyes are always best. Babies love faces and good eyes! Mouths that move are preferable. Remember to open the mouth each time the puppet says a word. Try not to move the puppet around too much so that your baby's eyes don't have to work too hard to follow the puppet.

6 MONTHS AND UP

Soft Plush Toys 	For developing senses. Playing with plush toys engages your baby's sense of touch with their fabric textures. Your infant will love to touch and feel these new textures. They can use their mouth with soft toys, which can provide the perfect mix for developing sensory skills and encouraging social and emotional growth. Some infants will begin to grasp the toys to feel the various sizes and textures. These soft toys are a perfect way for them to engage. **Please note:** for sense of touch, your baby does not have to be sitting upright (as shown in the photo) to feel the various textures.

Nesting Cups 	For hand and finger movement. Model for your baby how to stack or fit the *nesting cups* together. Your baby will eventually try different ways to take the cups apart and find what is best to use with both *hands*. As they get older (within their first year), they will be able to nest the cups together and stack by size. (Age may vary to acquire this skill.)
Musical Toys 	Encourage learning and hands-on play in such a fun way. You can introduce musical toys to your baby and model how to play with them. Eventually, as the months go on, your baby will develop the arm strength to play with the toys themselves.
Books (soft and hard; with colors, shapes, and animals)  	Good for eyesight and language development. Babies will be so entertained during bathtime with a colorful **soft bath book**. When out of the tub they will enjoy a **board book**, with its easy-to-turn pages. These durable books will not rip, even if your baby puts it in their mouth while teething. For a newborn, it's best to select books with high-contrast images. For older infants, look for books that require some manual dexterity, such as lift-the-flap books and touch-and-feel books. For infants, begin by holding and turning the pages of the book for them. *Read, read, and read to your baby!* Once your child develops more dexterity, let them hold the book while you read to them or as you walk them in their stroller.

Bath/Squeeze Toys 	For eyes, hands, and fingers. You can hold and squeak the toys, and as your baby gets older, they will be able to hold/grasp and squeak them too. These are great bath-time toys!
High-Chair Spinning Toys 	Suction-based toys easily attach to any tray surface and are great for entertaining your baby after they eat and while you enjoy your meal. Suction rattles are ideal for your baby to spin and swing, encouraging gross motor skills (movements your baby makes with their arms). High-chair toys make mealtime fun!
Sensory Ball 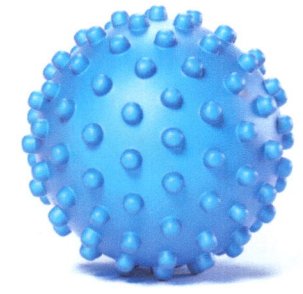	Four-inch, translucent sensory balls are perfect for developing your baby's tactile senses and gross motor skills. Baby may hold, squeeze, and peer through these textured play balls.

Establishing Baby-Safe Enrichment Areas in the Home

- The infant's bedroom or sleeping area should be cheerful and decorated at baby's eye level with black, white, and red images because of the bold, eye-catching colors with shapes and patterns. Pictures of people's faces, photos of children and their families, friendly animals, and other familiar objects are excellent choices.

- Easy-to-clean carpet is a good choice for the floors in the rooms where your baby will play. However, if you plan to have wooden or another type of flooring, then possibly have a mat or a throw rug just for additional textures for their feet. Allow your infant to go barefoot whenever possible to give their feet a chance to breathe and to allow their toes freedom of movement.

- Change the play area periodically throughout the day from the floor, to the stroller, to being carried, to rocking or swinging, and other variations to give infants different perspectives on people and places.

- Place baby-friendly mirrors where infants can observe themselves—for example, on the wall next to the floor or next to the diapering area/changing table.

- Arrange space so that babies can enjoy moments of quiet play with space to roll over and crawl toward interesting objects in their later months.

- Always supervise your baby both indoors and outdoors.

- Toys should be safe, washable, and large enough in size so they can't be swallowed.

- In the case of older infants, if you get any climbing structures, they should be low to the ground and steps should be provided. The structures should be well padded and safe for baby's exploration.

- Books should be heavy cardboard with rounded edges or cloth.

- Electrical outlets *must* be covered with plastic outlet covers (these are usually not costly). When your baby begins to crawl, they will be curious about the outlets (never let them touch when not covered). Most local big chain stores carry them in a pack or you can hire a baby proofing company to baby proof your outlets and different parts of your house. You can Google local companies for company information or get recommendations.

- Hazardous substances should *never* be within a child's reach.

- Extension cords should *never* be exposed.

- Babies should *never* be left alone or with any pet.

Learning Activities
(Newborn to 6 Months)

From the moment a baby is born, they love to play. Exploring with their mouth is a great way for your baby to learn, so let them do it as much as possible. Make sure all items they place in their mouth are clean and large enough in size so they can't be swallowed. (I can't stress this enough!) Even if your baby is months away from cutting their first tooth, teething toys in a variety of shapes, textures, and tastes are excellent enrichment tools at this stage.

Rolling a ball to your baby is a great way to offer your baby a physical challenge. Social games, such as peek-a-boo, are fun and stimulating. On the next several pages, you will find wonderful, age-appropriate infant activities that you and your baby can do together within their first year.

Please keep in mind that the following activities have an approximate and general age or range, so your baby may be able to do the activity earlier or later.

PLEASE NOTE: Every baby develops at a different pace, and that is okay.

Bubbles, Bubbles Everywhere

Age: Newborn & Up

Skill: Hand-eye coordination, seeing and reaching out to bubbles with hands (closer to 6 months and older for this skill).

Objective: To help your baby learn what their brain tells them as well as to discover some of their body parts.

Materials: Bubbles for blowing, Bouncer Seat, or Bathtub Seat

Activity: Get your baby settled in either a Bouncer Seat, bathtub seat (if during bath time), and then take out bubbles. Start by blowing a few gently in their direction, letting them reach out to them as they float by (and taking care not to get the soapy bubble formula in their eyes). Though they won't be able to catch the bubbles yet, they'll enjoy trying to grab for them. (Babies around the age of 4 months may begin grabbing for bubbles.) Then start aiming bubbles at his or her legs, arms, hands, tummy, and so on, naming each body part as you go up. For example, "There's some bubbles on your tummy!" and "There's a bubble on your hand!" If their skin is a little damp, the bubble may land without popping right away.

Can You Find It?

Age: Newborn & Up

Skill: Visual tracking: ability to follow a moving object with the eyes.

Objective: To engage your baby to follow a moving object with their eyes.

Materials: black and white pictures, your face, a basic toy or simple household object

Activity: Hold objects 6 to 12 inches in front of baby's face in the direction they are looking. Slowly move the object an inch or two in one direction. Newborns are just learning to follow moving objects with their eyes (called visual tracking), so wait for your baby to find the object and then move it a bit more.

Tummy Time!

Age: 3 Months & Up

Skill: Gross motor, which is the development of larger muscle movements that are responsible for running, jumping, and throwing. In infancy, crawling, lifting one's head, rolling over, and sitting up are examples of gross motor development.

Objective: To get your baby on their tummy and eventually to have them learn how to push up, roll over, sit up, crawl, and stand.

Materials: towel, mat (if no carpet) for baby to lie on, a book or an activity they can look at while on their tummy

Activity: Get down on the floor with your baby. Look them in the eyes as you lie on your own belly. Lay your baby down on a towel and use it to gently roll them from side to side. Try saying, "oops-a-daisy, uh-oh" or whichever word you like as you roll them. You can also put a board book open in front of your baby or place a favorite toy within reach. Buy a tummy-time toy, such as a plastic mirror with fabric backing (see page 23), or play activity mat, such as a brightly colored and interactive mat for your baby's playtime (see page 23). They come in lots of different sizes, shapes and themes but they all have small toys, designed especially for babies to play with while on their belly. Some have lights, mirrors, moving pictures, music and/or squeaky toys attached. Take your baby's socks off so they can get good traction on the mat, towel or carpet. Your baby will enjoy the ride!

Mirror, Mirror

Age: 3 months & Up

Skill: Baby observation of various facial expressions, strengthening neck and head muscles (Tummy Time).

Objective: To encourage your baby to notice their face in the mirror.

Materials: Mirror

Activity: Stand with both you and your little one looking into the mirror (your hands will be free if you have your baby in a front pack facing forward). Now make exaggerated faces with accompanying sounds. Lightly tap your baby's nose with your finger, making a popping sound each time. Hold out or wave baby's arms, then do the same with yours. Sway from side to side. Repeat several times.

Touch and Feel

Age: 3 Months & Up

Skill: Touch sensations: this helps baby interpret visual information and to help them learn about life and its surroundings.

Objective: To allow your baby to feel a variety of sensations.

Materials: Soft paintbrush, a hairbrush, ice cube, blow-dryer, soft blanket with satin (if you have one), very fine-grain sandpaper, feathers or cotton balls

Activity: Let your baby briefly feel the cold of an ice cube, as well as the warmth of a blow dryer from a safe distance (be careful not to make the air too warm; keep it on the lowest warm setting). Contrast the softness of a satin blanket with the roughness of sandpaper (be careful—not too rough). Say "warm" and "cold," "soft" and "hard" as you offer the different items. Continue with other materials and sensations.

Buzzing World of Words

Age: Between 3 & 12 months

Skill: Language acquisition, the beginning of language, the baby is playing around with the sounds of speech and sorting out the sounds that are important for making words in their *language.*

Objective: To engage your baby in listening to retain many words.

Materials: none

Activity: Your baby is listening intently to their surroundings at this age and soaking up this buzzing world of words. It is important to constantly talk to your baby during this time. One great way to do this is to describe what you are doing as you are doing it. For instance, "Now it's time to change your diaper . . . What a yucky diaper! Here I go . . . let's throw it out! Let's put on a new one . . ." and so on. Look at your baby as you tell them what you are doing. Babies begin to understand language long before they utter their first word. Continue to use other parts of your day to talk to your baby.

NOTE: Remember that quiet time is just as important to your baby. Use your judgment in this area by reading your baby's cues; you never want to overstimulate your baby.

Dancing to the Music

Age: Beginning About 5 or 6 Months

Skill: Helps with balance, gross and fine motor skills with head, neck, arm, and legs.

Objective: To give your baby a new perspective when carried upright by adding music.

Materials: Any music of your choice

Activity: Turn on the music and then hoist your baby onto your hip or higher on your body to what's comfortable. Hold your baby upright with one arm, and with your free hand hold theirs, as if you're dancing together. As you listen to the music, gently rock your hips back and forth, taking careful steps or turning in circles as the rhythm moves you. Sing along if you like.

Your baby will enjoy not only being close to you, but also the new view of things they can see from this height: for example, items on shelves and pictures on the wall. When the song ends, hold the baby under each arm and gently swing them in a circle.

Pop! Goes the Weasel

Age: About 6 Months

Skill: Repetition, turn-taking, and cause and effect (the relationship between an action and its outcome).

Objective: To help your baby understand that certain sounds mean what they sound like.

Materials: A *Jack in the Box* toy, a rattle, or stuffed animal

Activity: For the *Jack in the Box*, sing the classic nursery song "Pop! Goes the Weasel," (you can look up the words by doing a search on Google) but highlight the element of surprise with sound effects and actions.

Start out softly and slowly: for the *Jack in the Box*, crank the knob and keep turning it as you sing, "Round and round cobbler's bench, the monkey chased the weasel, the monkey thought 'twas all in fun . . . "—then raise your voice to finish—"Pop! Goes the Weasel."

You can try this again with the stuffed animal, clap your hands on the word "pop." Now sing it again, this time with a stuffed animal. Clap your hands lightly on the floor or a nearby padded surface such as a bed or chair. Next, make the stuffed animal jump up into the air on the word "pop."

This song can also work wonders as a distraction during diaper changes and is also great for keeping your baby awake on short car rides when you don't want them to nap just yet. If they seem startled rather than pleased when you get to the ending, tone it down a bit.

If using the rattle: Your baby can learn that shaking a rattle creates a sound as well; your baby can learn that also pressing certain buttons may make a toy light up or make a noise.

> **NOTE:** I know this is an old-fashioned song (even for me!), but it is an educational classic. It really is perfect for developing the skill listed. You can find the words and music on the Internet with a Google search or download an app with nursery rhymes.

Look Who's Here!

Age: About 6 Months

Skill: Sense of cause and effect, the relationship between an action and its outcome. Object permanence is the idea that even though the baby can't see something (like your smiling face), it still exists. Object permanence usually begins about 5 months.

Objective: To engage your baby in the delight of cause-and-effect responses.

Materials: Something for parent to hide behind (such as hands or blanket)

Activity: While your baby is on the changing table, but holding them at least with one hand (securely of course), dunk down below the side, then pop up with an exaggerated smile or round-eyed "surprise face" and see if you get a giggle out of them. As they get older and more used to the game, repeat it with different expressions on your face each time you reappear. This can go on until your facial muscles get tired. (If the baby starts to follow you as you bend down, that means they are too old and too smart for the game.) You can also play pop-up by poking your head out around doorways and corners in the house.

NOTE: Each baby develops at a different pace, so if your baby isn't quite ready for this activity, don't worry—just try it again in a few weeks.

Kicking Back

Age: Beginning at 6 months

Skill: Gross motor with regards to legs and arms, sense of cause and effect, which is the relationship between an action and its outcome.

Objective: To allow your baby to exercise their arms and legs.

Materials: A baby bathtub

Activity: Fill a small baby bathtub with 3 to 4 inches of water (no more than that). Hold your baby upright in a sitting position. Most babies love the stimulation of the water, and many will start kicking their legs happily. The more they kick, the higher the splashes, and they will discover that it's their legs that are causing all the splashing. Watch out!

NOTE: Never leave a baby unattended in water for even a moment.

Fostering Positive Qualities

The positive qualities discussed in the following chart become more important as your baby gets older, but you can begin fostering these qualities while your child is still an infant. They take time to learn and practice, so give your baby plenty of opportunities at home to begin developing these qualities. Ultimately, you want your child to have a great **SELF-ESTEEM**, confidence and satisfaction in oneself and is the ultimate goal for your child.

Confidence	A child must feel good about themselves and believe they can succeed. A confident child is more willing to attempt new tasks and try again if they do not succeed the first time.
Independence	A child must learn to do things for themselves.
Curiosity	A child is naturally curious and must remain so to get the most out of learning opportunities.
Motivation	A child must want to learn.
Persistence	A child must learn to finish what they start.
Cooperation	A child must be able to get along with others and learn to share and take turns.
Self-control	A child must learn that there are positive and negative ways to express anger. They must understand that some behaviors, such as hitting and biting, are not acceptable.
Empathy	A child must have an interest in others and understand how others feel.

To help your child develop these qualities, do the following (in some areas these examples are for when your baby gets older):

✓ **Show your child that you care about them and that you are dependable.** No matter your baby's age, feeling loved will likely help them to be confident. Your child must believe that, no matter what, someone will look out for them. Give your baby plenty of attention, encouragement, and hugs.

✓ **Set a good example.** Children imitate what they see others do and what they hear others say. When you exercise and eat nourishing food, your child is more likely to do so as well. When you treat others with respect, your child probably will too. If you share things with others, your child also will learn to be thoughtful of other's feelings and needs. It's never too soon to start modeling respectful, caring behaviors.

✓ **Provide opportunities for repetition.** It takes practice for a baby to learn to pronounce new sounds, use words, and hold a bottle or cup. Your child doesn't get bored when they repeat things. Instead, by repeating things until they learn them, your child builds the confidence they need to try new things.

✓ **Use appropriate discipline.** (This pertains to when your baby is beginning their toddler years—after the first year and up.) All children need to have limits set for them. Children whose parents give them firm but loving discipline generally develop better social skills and do better in school than do children whose parents set too few or too many limits.

✓ **Be positive and encouraging.** Praise your baby when they learn something new and older children for a job well done. Smiles and encouragement go much further to shape good behavior than harsh punishment.

✓ **Let your child do many things by themselves.** (This pertains to when your baby is beginning their toddler years—after the first year and up.) Young children need to be watched closely. However, they learn to be independent and to develop confidence by doing tasks such as dressing themselves and putting their toys away. It's important to let your child make choices, rather than deciding everything for them.

✓ **Encourage your child to play with other children and to be with adults who are not family members.** (This pertains to when your baby is beginning their toddler years—after the first year and up.) Especially when in preschool, children need social opportunities to learn to see the point of view of others.

✓ **Show a positive attitude toward learning and toward school.** (This pertains to when your baby is beginning their toddler years—after the first year and up.) Children come into this world with a powerful need to discover and to explore. If your child is to keep their curiosity, you need to encourage it and show enthusiasm for what your child does (for example, "You've drawn a great picture!"). Encouragement and enthusiasm help to make them proud of their achievements.

Age-Appropriate Storybooks
(Newborn to 6 Months & Older)

For 3 to 6 months, we recommend only board books and soft bath books. Suggested books include:

- *Baby Bathtime!* by Dawn Sirett
- *Baby Faces* by DK Publishing
- *Baby: Colors* by DK Publishing
- *Big Fat Hen* by Keith Baker
- *Brown Bear, Brown Bear What Do You See?* by Bill Martin Jr./Eric Carle
- *Colors and Shapes* by DK Publishing
- *Counting Kisses* by Karen Katz
- *Goodnight Moon* by Margaret Wise Brown
- *Guess How Much I Love You* by Sam McBratney
- *Hide and Seek First Words* by DK Publishing
- *I Went Walking* by Sue Williams
- *Jamberry* by Bruce Degen

- *Moo, Baa, La La La!* by Sandra Boynton
- *Mr. Brown Can Moo, Can You?* by Dr. Seuss
- *My First Numbers* by DK Publishing
- *Pat the Bunny* by Dorothy Kunhardt
- *Polar Bear, Polar Bear, What Do You Hear?* by Bill Martin Jr./Eric Carle
- *The Rainbow Fish* by Marcus Pfister
- *Tickle, Tickle* by Helen Oxen bury
- *Touch and Feel Animals* by DK Publishing
- *Where Is Baby's Belly Button?* by Karen Katz
- *Where's Spot?* by Eric Hill
- *White on Black* by Tana Hoban

NOTE: These books are some of my favorites and classics that I shared with my children when they were babies. There are many other wonderful books to choose from, so you can find your own favorites.

For other recommended items & educational toys to keep in your home, please visit facebook.com/mySmartChild and Instagram@mySmartChild

To Sum It All Up

You have come to end of this SmartGuide, and I hope you learned more about your baby's developmental needs, your role in your baby's life and education, and how you can enrich your infant's environment. Incorporating the tips, suggestions, and activities in this book into your baby's daily life is the first step in building a solid foundation for your child's accomplishments throughout life.

Revisit the information in this SmartGuide from time to time to keep these ideas fresh in your mind. Your baby's development and growth will amaze you. However, please don't be discouraged if your baby is not achieving a specific skill at a specific time. With continued practice, encouragement, and love, it should come naturally in the appropriate time. With this SmartGuide of information at your fingertips, your baby will always be "one step ahead."

> We now offer VIRTUAL one on one or group parent sessions. For further information or questions, please visit us on social media and make an appointment for a FREE parent consultation.

Remember:
A smart learning path begins at home.

TESTIMONIALS

"Bonnie Rosenstein is not only an academic in infant learning, she is also well practiced, having raised two smart, fun-loving, and high-character children. Bonnie has made it her mission in life to help others help their kids. In her book, she leaves no stone unturned, providing countless golden parenting nuggets on how to get a jumpstart on your child's learning. And she does it in a conversational way, making it as easy as one, two, three."

—MIKE WHALEN, Partner, Goodwin Procter LLP

"My twins were fortunate enough to have Bonnie Chall Rosenstein as a Preschool teacher. She set the bar high for them and they grabbed it! I truly believe that their first classroom experience with "Miss Bonnie" prepared them for their love of learning, which lasted through college. They soaked up her lessons like little sponges, learned so much and were more than ready for kindergarten. Our family will always be grateful to Bonnie Chall Rosenstein for making it fun to be smart!"

—CATHY HARTNEY, mom of twins Chelsea & Ryan

"As the Education Director, Bonnie coordinated programs for elementary schools and preschool safety fairs. These events focused on the health and safety of infants and children by educating them and their parents about safety in and out of the home. Bonnie was also an amazing advocate for bicycle and pedestrian safety through public and private schools across the state of Florida. Her efforts created awareness for the safety of our youth."

—TARA APPLEBAUM, Life Coach, Consultant, Road Safety Advocate

About Bonnie Rosenstein, M.A. Ed.

Bonnie Rosenstein obtained her certification in Elementary Education with a Bachelor of Science from the University of Hartford and a Master of Arts from Adelphi University. She has more than twenty years' teaching experience in the education field from infants up through sixth grade. She has been a pre-kindergarten teacher in various preschools and developed and executed a "Learning to Read" program, and most of the students were reading by the end of pre-kindergarten. She taught several grades in elementary school, wrote children's computer software programs for a start-up Internet company, and was instrumental in the setup and development where she worked her way up from a teacher to a directorship position of a Corporate Back-up Childcare Center for several years.

Bonnie's greatest experience has been raising her own two children. From the time her children were newborns, she engaged them in various enrichment activities and documented everything she and her children did. Other parents turned to her for advice about how and what to do to with their children to educate and enrich them. Bonnie's husband, Rich, inspired, motivated, and encouraged her to gather all her research and information to help other parents, which is how mySmartChild was created.

Both of Bonnie's children have been in gifted and honors courses, and taken college-level classes in high school. They have consistently succeeded at a significantly above-average rate in their subject areas. The support and educational foundation they received at home gave them what they needed to succeed in public school and college. Though her children have worked independently for some time, and have enjoyed excellent academic success, Bonnie has remained a part of both children's education, activities, and work-related endeavors. She and her husband, Rich, have always encouraged them to pursue their passions in hopes of succeeding in their greatest life pursuits.

Originally from New York, Bonnie currently lives in South Florida. She keeps up to date with current educational research and trends. She is truly passionate about a child's early learning at home prior to entering preschool or kindergarten. She knows that with the right tools and information, new parents can ensure that their babies will be on a very nurturing and educational path. For questions, concerns, or advice, visit us on social media and look for other age-related SmartGuides, educational products, and ideas.

> Don't forget to ask about a virtual one-on-one or group parent session. *For further information, visit* facebook.com/mySmartChild *or* Instagram@mySmartChild. *Make an appointment today for a FREE consultation.*

Our Family Then

Our Family Now

www.ingramcontent.com/pod-product-compliance
Lightning Source LLC
Chambersburg PA
CBHW060821090426
42738CB00002B/60